THE COLORS OF FRIENDSHIP

The Colors of Friendship

Learning About Autism with Ethan

Kimberly Medeiros

Kimberly Medeiros

CONTENTS

INTRODUCTION

Introduction

Ethan was a young boy who saw the world in a special way. While other children saw a simple blue sky, Ethan saw it filled with swirling shades of azure and sapphire. The grass wasn't just green to Ethan; it was a mix of emerald, jade, and lime.

Ethan had autism, which meant he experienced the world differently from most kids. Sounds were louder, lights were brighter, and feelings were often much bigger for him. But one thing that always made Ethan happy was his love for art.

Every day, Ethan spent hours with his sketchbook and paints. He loved creating vibrant pictures of the world as he saw it, full of colors and patterns that danced off the page. His favorite painting was of a rainbow, each color blending into the next with a burst of brightness that made him smile.

Despite his love for art, there was one thing Ethan wished for more than anything: to make friends at his new school. He imagined sharing his drawings with other kids and having someone to play with during recess. Ethan hoped that at this new school, he would find friends who understood and appreciated him for who he was.

1

First Day of School

The sun was just beginning to rise, casting a warm golden light over Ethan's room as he got ready for his first day at his new school. His backpack was filled with fresh supplies, and his favorite sketchbook was safely tucked inside. But as excited as Ethan was, he couldn't help feeling a flutter of nerves in his stomach.

"Are you ready, Ethan?" his mom called from downstairs.

Ethan took a deep breath and nodded, even though his mom couldn't see him. He picked up his backpack and headed down to the kitchen, where his parents were waiting with encouraging smiles.

"Remember, Ethan," his dad said as he ruffled Ethan's hair, "just be yourself. You have so much to offer, and we're sure you'll make some great friends."

Ethan's mom knelt down to his level and looked into his eyes. "And don't forget, if things feel too overwhelming, it's okay to take a break. You're going to do amazing things today, just like you always do with your art."

Their words filled Ethan with a little more confidence. He hugged his parents tightly before stepping out the door. As he walked to school, he tried to focus on the beautiful colors of the morning sky, imagining the new adventures and friends that might await him. He was nervous, but also hopeful. Today was a new beginning, and he was ready to embrace it

2

Meeting New Faces

As Ethan walked into his new classroom, he was greeted by a chorus of voices and the bustling energy of children settling in for the day. His teacher, Mrs. Garcia, smiled warmly and introduced him to the class.

"Class, this is Ethan. He's joining us today, and I know you'll all make him feel very welcome."

Ethan felt a dozen pairs of eyes on him, and his heart beat a little faster. He took a deep breath, remembering his parents' words. As he made his way to an empty desk, some of his new classmates whispered to each other, curious about the new boy. Others glanced at him but quickly returned to their own conversations, unsure of how to approach him.

Just as Ethan was settling into his seat, a cheerful voice called out, "Hi, Ethan! I'm Leo!"

Ethan looked up to see a boy with bright, friendly eyes and a big grin standing next to him. Leo was holding a colorful notebook and a pencil, looking eager to make a new friend.

"Do you like drawing?" Leo asked, noticing Ethan's sketchbook peeking out of his backpack.

Ethan nodded shyly. "I love drawing," he said softly.

"That's awesome!" Leo replied. "I like drawing, too. Maybe we can draw together sometime?"

Ethan's nerves began to ease as he felt the warmth of Leo's kindness. "I'd like that," he said, smiling back.

Throughout the day, Leo stayed close to Ethan, introducing him to other classmates and helping him navigate the new environment. While some kids were still unsure how to interact with Ethan, Leo's outgoing nature and friendly spirit made Ethan feel welcomed and less alone.

By the end of the day, Ethan felt a small spark of hope. He had met someone who seemed to understand him and wanted to be his friend. It was a good start to what he hoped would be a wonderful journey at his new school.

3

Initial Struggles

As the day progressed, Ethan found himself becoming more and more overwhelmed by the noise and activity in the classroom. The buzz of conversations, the clatter of pencils, and the scraping of chairs felt like a whirlwind of sound swirling around him.

During a group activity, Ethan sat at his desk, feeling the pressure of the noise building in his head. His hands instinctively went to his ears, trying to block out the overwhelming sounds. The unfamiliar routines and loud environment were making it hard for him to concentrate or feel comfortable.

Leo, who was sitting nearby, noticed Ethan's distress. He saw his new friend covering his ears and looking visibly upset. Leo remembered how much Ethan loved art and how calm and happy he seemed when they talked about drawing.

Without hesitation, Leo leaned over to Mrs. Garcia and whispered something in her ear. She nodded and walked over to Ethan.

"Ethan," Mrs. Garcia said gently, "I can see that the noise is a bit much for you right now. Would you like to take a break and go to the art corner? It's quieter there, and you can draw if you'd like."

Ethan looked up, relief washing over him. He nodded gratefully and stood up, making his way to the quiet corner of the classroom that was filled with art supplies and a cozy reading nook.

Leo followed him, carrying his own notebook. "Can I join you?" he asked.

Ethan smiled and nodded, feeling grateful for Leo's understanding and support. As they sat together in the peaceful corner, Ethan picked up his sketchbook and began to draw. The noise of the classroom faded away, replaced by the soothing strokes of his pencil on paper.

Leo watched Ethan's hand move gracefully across the page, creating a beautiful picture of a serene landscape. "That's amazing, Ethan," he said. "You're really talented."

Ethan looked up, his anxiety melting away in the presence of his new friend. "Thanks, Leo. Drawing helps me feel better."

Leo smiled. "I'm glad. And I'm happy to have a friend who can teach me how to see the world in such a colorful way."

In that moment, Ethan realized that with friends like Leo, he could find ways to navigate the challenges of his new school. With support and understanding, he could turn overwhelming moments into opportunities to share his unique perspective with others.

4

As the school day went on, Leo and Ethan continued to spend time together. During a quiet moment in the classroom, Leo turned to Ethan with a thoughtful look on his face.

"Ethan," Leo began hesitantly, "can I ask you something?"

Ethan looked up from his sketchbook and nodded. "Sure, what is it?"

"Well," Leo said, choosing his words carefully, "sometimes you do things a little differently from the other kids. Like when you cover your ears or when you need to take a break. I was wondering why that is."

Ethan paused, thinking about how to explain. He wanted Leo to understand him better. "I have something called autism," he said finally. "It means that I experience the world differently from most people."

Leo listened intently, his eyes full of curiosity and concern. "What do you mean by 'differently'?"

"Sometimes noises that don't bother other people feel really loud and overwhelming to me," Ethan explained. "And sometimes, if there's a lot going on, I need extra time to understand everything. It's like my brain is super busy, and I need to take a break to sort things out."

Leo nodded slowly. "So, when you cover your ears, it's because the noise is too much?"

"Exactly," Ethan said, feeling relieved that Leo was listening so carefully. "And when I take breaks, it helps me feel calm again. Everyone's brain works a little differently, and mine just needs different things to feel okay."

Leo thought about this for a moment. "That makes sense," he said. "Thanks for explaining it to me, Ethan. I want to make sure I can be a good friend and help you if you need it."

Ethan smiled, feeling a deep sense of gratitude. "Thanks, Leo. It means a lot to me that you want to understand."

Leo grinned back. "Of course! And if you ever need to take a break or if something is too loud, just let me know. I'll help however I can."

In that moment, Ethan realized that he had found a true friend in Leo—someone who not only accepted his differences but also wanted to understand and support him. It made the challenges he faced feel a little less daunting, knowing that he didn't have to face them alone.

From then on, whenever Ethan felt overwhelmed, Leo was there to offer a reassuring smile or a quiet place to sit together. Their friendship grew stronger, built on a foundation of understanding and acceptance. And as they navigated the ups and downs of school life together, they discovered that their differences only made their friendship more special and unique.

5

When the bell rang for recess, the classroom erupted with excitement as the children rushed outside to play. Ethan, feeling the need for some quiet time, grabbed his sketchbook and headed towards a secluded corner of the playground. He found a shady spot under a big oak tree and settled down, opening his sketchbook to a fresh page.

As he began to draw, the world around him seemed to fade away. The familiar comfort of his pencil moving across the paper helped him relax. He lost himself in the swirling colors and intricate patterns that flowed from his imagination.

A few minutes later, Ethan heard footsteps approaching. He looked up to see Leo standing nearby, a curious expression on his face.

"Hey, Ethan," Leo said, sitting down beside him. "What are you drawing?"

Ethan hesitated for a moment, then turned his sketchbook so Leo could see. On the page was a beautiful garden filled with vibrant flowers, each petal and leaf detailed with care.

"Wow, that's incredible!" Leo exclaimed. "You're really talented. How do you come up with all these ideas?"

Ethan smiled, feeling a warm glow inside. "I just draw what I see in my mind. It helps me feel calm and happy."

Leo nodded thoughtfully. "I like drawing too, but I'm not as good as you. Can you show me how you do it?"

Ethan's eyes lit up. He rarely had the chance to share his love for art with others. "Sure, I'd love to," he said.

He handed Leo a spare piece of paper and a pencil. Together, they started to draw, with Ethan guiding Leo on how to blend colors and create different textures. They laughed and talked, sharing stories and learning from each other.

As they drew, some of the other kids noticed and came over to see what was happening. At first, they just watched, but soon they started asking questions and complimenting Ethan's artwork.

"That's so cool!" one of the kids said. "Can you teach us too?"

Ethan looked around at the smiling faces and nodded. "Of course," he said, feeling a newfound confidence. "We can all draw together."

And so, under the big oak tree, a small group of children gathered, each one learning to see the world through Ethan's artistic lens. The quiet corner of the playground became a place of creativity and connection, where differences were celebrated and new friendships began to blossom.

As the recess bell rang, signaling the end of their break, Ethan felt a sense of accomplishment. He had not only found a friend in Leo but also discovered a way to connect with others through his passion for art. For the first time in a long while, Ethan felt truly hopeful about his new school and the friendships he was beginning to form.

6

As the days went by, Ethan found himself facing moments of overwhelm and misunderstanding. Sometimes, the noise in the classroom became too much, and he would cover his ears to block it out. Other times, he struggled to keep up with the fast pace of conversations or understand social cues.

During one particularly challenging day, Ethan felt tears welling up in his eyes as he sat at his desk, feeling isolated and alone. He wished he could make the world understand how he felt inside.

Leo noticed Ethan's distress and immediately sprang into action. Sensing his friend's need for support, he approached Ethan with a gentle smile.

"Hey, Ethan, are you okay?" Leo asked softly, placing a comforting hand on his shoulder.

Ethan looked up, feeling grateful for Leo's presence. "I'm just feeling a little overwhelmed," he admitted quietly.

Leo nodded understandingly. "I get it. Sometimes things can feel really hard. But you're not alone, Ethan. I'm here for you, and so are the rest of us."

With Leo's encouragement, Ethan felt a glimmer of hope. He took a deep breath and wiped away his tears, knowing that his friend had his back.

As the day went on, Leo stood by Ethan's side, helping others understand and adapt to Ethan's needs. He explained to their classmates that sometimes Ethan needed a quiet space or extra time to process things. He showed them how to offer support and understanding instead of judgment or confusion.

Slowly but surely, Ethan began to feel more accepted and understood. His classmates started to adapt to his differences, offering him a kind word or a reassuring smile when he needed it most.

And through it all, Leo remained by Ethan's side, a steadfast beacon of support and friendship. With his help, Ethan faced each challenge with courage and resilience, knowing that no matter what, he had a friend who would always stand by him.

Together, Ethan and Leo showed their classmates that empathy and understanding could bridge the gap between differences, creating a community where everyone felt valued and included. And as they faced each new day together, Ethan knew that with Leo by his side, there was nothing they couldn't overcome.

7

Ethan and Leo sat under the oak tree, their sketchbooks open in front of them. Ethan turned to a page filled with a burst of colors—blues, greens, and purples swirling together to form a peaceful ocean scene.

"Wow, Ethan, that's amazing," Leo said, his eyes wide with admiration. "How do you decide what to draw?"

Ethan smiled shyly. "Well, I use colors to show how I'm feeling. Like, if I'm happy, I use bright colors like yellow and orange. When I'm feeling calm, I draw things like the ocean with cool colors like blue and green."

Leo nodded, fascinated. "That's so cool. So, this ocean means you were feeling calm?"

"Yeah," Ethan replied. "Drawing helps me express my feelings, especially when it's hard to say them out loud."

Leo picked up his pencil and looked at Ethan's drawing again. "Can you teach me how to draw like that? I want to learn how to use colors to show my feelings too."

Ethan felt a surge of excitement. He had never had a chance to teach someone his way of drawing before. "Sure, I'd love to," he said. "Let's start with something simple. How about we draw a tree together?"

Leo nodded eagerly. "Okay!"

Ethan began by sketching the outline of a tree, explaining each step as he went. "First, we draw the trunk. It's like the tree's body. Then we add the branches, which are like its arms reaching out."

Leo followed along, carefully copying Ethan's lines. "Got it," he said, concentrating hard.

"Now for the fun part," Ethan said with a smile. "Let's use colors to make the tree come alive. If the tree is in the spring, we can use bright green for the leaves. If it's autumn, we can use reds, oranges, and yellows."

Leo picked up a green pencil and started coloring his tree. "I think my tree is in the summer," he said. "What about yours?"

Ethan thought for a moment, then chose a mix of warm colors. "I'm going to make mine an autumn tree," he said. "I love the way the leaves look when they change colors."

As they colored, Ethan explained more about how different colors made him feel. "Red can mean strong feelings, like excitement or anger. Blue can be calm or sometimes a little sad. And yellow is happy, like sunshine."

Leo listened carefully, trying to understand how colors could express so many different emotions. "This is really cool, Ethan. I never thought about colors like that before."

Ethan felt a warm glow of pride. "I'm glad you like it. Drawing and colors help me a lot. It's like speaking a special language."

By the time the recess bell rang, Leo had a colorful tree in his sketchbook, and Ethan had a new friend who appreciated his unique way of seeing the world. As they walked back to class, Leo held up his drawing proudly.

"Thanks for teaching me, Ethan. I can't wait to do more drawings with you."

Ethan smiled, feeling more connected and understood than ever before. "Me too, Leo. Me too."

8

Leo sat quietly for a moment, taking in everything Ethan had shared. He wanted to make sure he truly understood. "So, Ethan," Leo began, "does having autism change the way you see other things too? Like, do you notice things differently?"

Ethan nodded, appreciating Leo's genuine curiosity. "Yeah, I do. Sometimes I notice details that other people might miss. Like the way light reflects off a leaf or the patterns in the clouds. It can be really beautiful."

Leo smiled. "That sounds amazing. I guess it's like you have a superpower for seeing all the special details in the world."

Ethan blushed a little, not used to thinking about his autism in such a positive light. "I never thought of it that way, but I guess you're right."

Leo leaned forward, his expression serious but kind. "I'm really glad you told me about this, Ethan. Everyone has their own unique way of seeing the world. That's what makes each of us special."

Ethan felt a wave of relief and gratitude. "Thanks, Leo. It feels good to talk about it with someone who wants to understand."

Leo nodded. "I'm always here to listen. And if there's anything I can do to help, just let me know. We're friends, and friends support each other."

Ethan smiled, feeling more at ease than he had in a long time. "You're a really good friend, Leo."

Leo grinned back. "And you're a really good friend too, Ethan. I'm lucky to know you."

Their conversation left Ethan feeling more understood and accepted. He realized that with friends like Leo, he could navigate the challenges of school and life more confidently. Knowing that someone saw his differences as strengths made all the difference.

From that day on, Leo and Ethan's friendship grew stronger. Leo continued to ask questions and show interest in Ethan's experiences, and Ethan found comfort in sharing his unique perspective with someone who cared. Together, they learned from each other and discovered that everyone's way of seeing the world was valuable.

Through their friendship, Ethan and Leo taught their classmates that understanding and empathy could build bridges between people, no matter how different they might seem. And in the colorful tapestry of their friendship, each thread, no matter how unique, added to the beauty and richness of their shared experiences.

9

One sunny afternoon, as recess approached, Leo turned to Ethan with a twinkle in his eye. "Hey, Ethan, a bunch of us are going to play soccer. Do you want to join us?"

Ethan hesitated, his mind racing with doubts and worries. Soccer was a fast-paced game with lots of movement and noise—things that often made him feel overwhelmed. But then he remembered Leo's reassuring smile and the support he had shown him in the past.

Taking a deep breath, Ethan nodded. "Okay, I'll give it a try."

Leo's face lit up with excitement. "That's awesome! Come on, let's go join the others."

As they made their way to the soccer field, Ethan felt a mix of nerves and anticipation. He was stepping out of his comfort zone, but with Leo by his side, he knew he wasn't alone.

When they reached the field, the other kids greeted them warmly. Ethan recognized some familiar faces from his class and felt a small spark of confidence.

Leo grabbed a soccer ball and passed it to Ethan. "You can be on my team," he said with a grin. "We'll make a great team together."

Ethan felt a surge of gratitude for Leo's unwavering support. With his friend by his side, he felt a little braver.

As the game began, Ethan focused on the ball, trying to block out the noise and chaos around him. Leo stayed close, offering encouragement and guidance whenever Ethan needed it.

At first, Ethan struggled to keep up with the fast-paced action, but with each pass and kick, he felt more comfortable. He started to relax, letting the rhythm of the game guide him.

And then, something amazing happened. Ethan intercepted a pass and dribbled the ball down the field, his heart pounding with excitement. With a swift kick, he sent the ball soaring into the goal, scoring a point for his team.

The other kids cheered and high-fived Ethan, their faces lit up with smiles. Ethan couldn't believe it—he had scored a goal!

Leo ran over and wrapped Ethan in a tight hug. "You did it, Ethan! That was amazing!"

Ethan grinned from ear to ear, feeling a rush of pride and joy. He had stepped out of his comfort zone and tried something new, and it had paid off in the best possible way.

As they continued to play, Ethan felt more and more confident. With Leo's support and encouragement, he discovered that he was capable of more than he had ever imagined.

And as the sun began to set on the soccer field, Ethan knew that with friends like Leo by his side, there was nothing he couldn't do. Together, they had conquered their fears and embraced a new adventure, showing the world that true friendship knows no bounds.

10

One day, Mrs. Garcia announced an exciting class project: creating a mural that would represent their unique personalities and interests. Ethan's heart raced with excitement at the thought of using art to bring their class together.

As the class gathered around the blank canvas, Ethan stepped forward, feeling a surge of determination. "I have an idea," he said, his voice strong and confident. "Let's use colors and shapes to represent each of us. That way, our mural will reflect the diversity and beauty of our class."

The other children listened intently, curious to hear Ethan's plan. With Leo's encouragement, they began brainstorming ideas and sketching rough outlines on the canvas.

One by one, each child added their own unique touch to the mural. Some used bold, vibrant colors to represent their outgoing personalities, while others chose softer shades to reflect their quiet strength. Shapes of all sizes and styles emerged on the canvas, each one a reflection of the person who created it.

As they worked, Ethan guided his classmates, offering advice and encouragement. He showed them how to blend colors to create new shades and how to use different brush strokes to add texture and depth to their designs.

Leo joined in eagerly, his enthusiasm infectious. He helped organize the materials and offered ideas for incorporating everyone's strengths into the mural.

As the mural began to take shape, Mrs. Garcia watched with pride, amazed by the creativity and collaboration of her students. She saw children who had once felt isolated or misunderstood coming together as a unified team, learning from each other's strengths and celebrating their differences.

And as the final brush strokes were added to the mural, a sense of accomplishment filled the classroom. The children stood back to admire their work, their faces beaming with pride.

"This mural is amazing," one of the kids exclaimed. "It's like a reflection of all of us."

Ethan smiled, feeling a swell of happiness in his chest. With Leo and his classmates by his side, he had helped create something beautiful—a testament to the power of friendship, teamwork, and the limitless possibilities that come from embracing each other's differences.

As they admired their masterpiece, Ethan knew that their mural was more than just a work of art. It was a symbol of unity and inclusivity, a reminder that when they worked together, there was nothing they couldn't achieve. And with friends like Leo and his classmates, Ethan knew that the future was filled with endless possibilities.

With the final brushstroke, the mural was complete—a vibrant tapestry of colors, shapes, and textures that celebrated the unity and diversity of their class.

As the children stepped back to admire their masterpiece, a sense of awe filled the room. Each brushstroke told a story, capturing the essence of their individual personalities and strengths. It was a true reflection of the beautiful mosaic that made up their class.

Mrs. Garcia smiled with pride as she looked at her students. "This mural is truly incredible," she said, her voice filled with admiration. "It represents the unity and diversity that make our class so special."

The children cheered, their faces glowing with excitement and pride. They had worked tirelessly together, overcoming challenges and embracing each other's differences to create something truly remarkable.

To celebrate their achievement, Mrs. Garcia organized a small celebration in the classroom. She brought out snacks and drinks, and the children gathered around the mural, sharing stories and laughter.

One by one, they took turns sharing what the mural meant to them. Some spoke of the friendships they had formed, while others talked about the joy of working together as a team. Each story was a testament to the power of unity and collaboration.

Ethan stood among his classmates, feeling a swell of happiness in his heart. He looked at the mural, his eyes tracing the vibrant colors and intricate patterns. It was more than just a work of art—it was a symbol of friendship, acceptance, and the beauty found in diversity.

As the celebration came to an end, Mrs. Garcia announced that the mural would be proudly displayed in the school hallway for all to see. It would serve as a reminder of the incredible journey they had embarked on together—a journey filled with laughter, learning, and love.

And as the children said their goodbyes and headed home for the day, Ethan knew that the memories they had created would stay with them forever. With the mural as a symbol of their unity and diversity, their class would continue to inspire others to embrace each other's differences and celebrate the beauty found in every color of the rainbow.

12

As Ethan sat in his room that evening, he couldn't help but smile as he thought about the events of the day. The completion of the mural, the celebration with his classmates —it had been a day filled with laughter, joy, and a deep sense of accomplishment.

Looking around at the colorful drawings scattered across his desk, Ethan felt a surge of gratitude for the friendships he had formed. He had found friends who appreciated him for who he was, quirks and all. And at the center of it all was Leo, his steadfast companion and unwavering supporter.

Ethan picked up a drawing he had done earlier that day—a simple sketch of him and Leo standing side by side, their arms linked in friendship. As he looked at the drawing, he realized how much their friendship had grown over the past few weeks.

Leo had been there for him through thick and thin, offering encouragement and understanding when Ethan needed it most. He had shown Ethan that true friendship knew no bounds—that it embraced differences and celebrated the unique qualities that made each person special.

And as Ethan reflected on their friendship, he knew that he was lucky to have someone like Leo by his side. Together, they had faced challenges and overcome obstacles, but through it all, their bond had only grown stronger.

As he placed the drawing back on his desk, Ethan made a silent promise to himself—to cherish their friendship and to always be there for Leo, just as Leo had been there for him.

With a sense of contentment and gratitude filling his heart, Ethan drifted off to sleep, knowing that no matter what tomorrow brought, he had a friend who would stand by him through it all.

And as the stars twinkled outside his window, Ethan dreamed of the adventures that lay ahead, knowing that with Leo by his side, anything was possible. For true friendship, he had learned, was the greatest treasure of all.

13

Conclusion

Dear Readers,

As you journey through the pages of this story, I invite you to reflect on the beauty found in diversity and the power of true friendship.

In a world where differences can sometimes divide us, it's important to remember that each person brings something unique and valuable to the table. Whether it's a different way of seeing the world, a unique talent, or a special perspective, our differences enrich our lives and make our communities stronger.

Friendship knows no bounds—it transcends differences in background, personality, and abilities. Just as Ethan and Leo discovered, true friendship embraces each other's differences and celebrates the beauty found in every individual.

So let us celebrate and understand the differences in everyone we meet. Let us open our hearts and minds to the richness of diversity and the magic of true friendship. For it is our unique qualities that make the world a more beautiful place, and it is through understanding and acceptance that we can create a brighter future for all.

With warmest wishes,
Kimberly Medeiros